CW00762712

1 MONTH OF
FREE
READING

at
www.ForgottenBooks.com

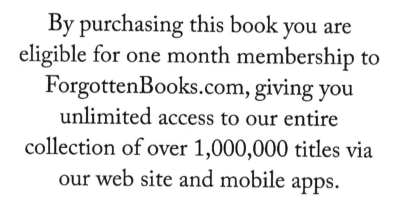

By purchasing this book you are eligible for one month membership to ForgottenBooks.com, giving you unlimited access to our entire collection of over 1,000,000 titles via our web site and mobile apps.

To claim your free month visit:
www.forgottenbooks.com/free910751

ISBN 978-0-265-92540-9
PIBN 10910751

CHEAP CLEARANCE LIST

OF

UNITED STATES AND FOREIGN COINS.

For Sale by CHAS. STEIGERWALT,

130 East King Street, Lancaster, Pa.

No. 21.　　　　ESTABLISHED 1878.　　　　SEPTEMBER, 1890.

REMARKS.

Please Read. Send orders early to prevent disappointment. Do not order any-thing you have not a reasonable expectation of buying if found correct, and return anything not desired as soon as possible after receipt of goods. Some of the coins, etc., in this list are out on approval now, but are included, as they may be returned. Coins sent on approval to responsible buyers. Remittances should be made by Postal Order, Postal Note, Registered Letter, Check or Draft. Don't send stamps of high values. Address all letters plainly, and make money orders, etc., payable to Chas. Steigerwalt, 130 East King Street, Lancaster, Pa.

Note. The prices of coins, etc., in this list have been marked extremely low, mostly at or below cost, that they may be sold as soon as possible to clear stock, and for this reason *no discounts will be made* either on large or small amounts. After the piece catalogued has been sold, no duplicate can be supplied at same price. Read the Catalogue carefully, as it is full of bargains.

CATALOGUE.

U. S. Gold Coins.

1800. Eagle. Exceedingly fine. 15.00
1800. Half Eagle. Extremely fine. 6.50.
1802. Half Eagle. Uncirculated. 7.00.
1803. Half Eagle. Very good. 6.00.
1806. Half Eagle. Extremely fine. 6.50.
1813. Half Eagle. About uncirculated. 7.00.
1859. Three Dollars. Very fine. 3.50.
1863. Three Dollars. About uncirculated. 4.50.
1804. Quarter Eagle. Extremely fine. 8.00.
1807. Quarter Eagle. Fine. 4.00.
1831. Quarter Eagle. Uncirculated. 5.00
1874. Quarter Eagle. Brilliant proof. 3.50.
1876. Quarter Eagle. Brilliant proof. 4.00.
1887. Quarter Eagle. Brilliant proof. 3.50.
Carolina Dollar. A. Bechtler. 27 G. 21 C. Very good. 1.50.

U. S. Dollars.

1794. Very good. Bold. A few light pin scratches. 60.00.
1795. Flowing hair. Very good and strong. 2.50.
1795. Fillet head. Very good. 2.50.
1796. Small date. Very good. 3.00.
1797. Seven stars facing. Very good. 3.00.
1797. Six stars facing. Very good. 3.00.
1798. *Thirteen stars. Small eagle.* Very fair. 3.00.
1798. Large eagle. Very good. 1.75.
1799. *Five stars facing.* Good. 3.50.

1799. Very good. 1.65.
1799 over '98· Very good. 1.65.
1800. Very good. 2.00.
1801. Very good. 2.25.
1802 over '01· Fine. 2.50.
1802. Very good. 2.25.
1803. Very good. 2.25.
1836. Worn, but everything plain. 3.50.
1841. Barely circulated. Lustre. 1.50.
1844. Good. 1.20.
1848. Very good. 1.30.
1852. Circulated, but still about good. A hole above the head has been plugged.
　　 20.00.
1853. Fine. 1.50.
1854. Very fine. 7.50.
1855. Very good. 4.00. Very good, but plugged through one star. 2.00.
1856. Very good. 1.50.
1857. Very fine. 2.00.
1858. Shows considerable circulation, but still about good (the only piece I have
　　 seen in this condition). 25.00.
1861. Uncirculated. 1.25.
1864. Brilliant proof, light haymarks. 1.75.
1866. Brilliant proof. 1.75.
1870. Proof. 1.35.
1871. Proof. 1.35.
1873. Dull proof. 1.25.
1878 Standard. 8 feathers in tail. Uncir'd; semi-proof. 1.35.
1879, 1880, 1881, 1884 Standard. Brilliant proofs. Lot. 4.75.
1880. Standard. S. mint. Uncirculated. 1.50.
1879. Trade. Brilliant proof. 1.65.
1880. Trade. Brilliant proof. 1.35.

U. S. Half Dollars.

1794. Good. 2.50.
1794. Very fair, date weak but visible. 1.00.
1794. Good but pierced through 79 of date. 1.00.
1795. Very good. 1.00.
1797. Very fair, date good, but has been plugged at point of bust. 20.00.
1801. Good. 2.00. Good but pierced. 1.00.
1802. Good. 3.50.
1803. Fine. 1.00. Very good. .75.
1805. Very good. .75.
1805 over '04· Very good. Rare. 3.00.
1806. No stem to wreath Fine. 1.00.
1806. Blunt and pointed 6. Very good. .75.
1807. Heads to right and left. Very good. .75.

1808 over '07. Fine. 1.00.
1808, 1809, 1810, 1811, 1812, 1813, 1814. Very good. .75.
1814 over '11. Fine. Scarce. 1.00.
1815. Good. 3.00.
1817 over '13. Very good. .85.
1829 over '21. Fine. .75.
1836. *Milled edge.* Very good. 2.50.
1836.' *Milled edge.* Good, but long scratch before face. 1.50.
1851. O. Mint. Extra fine. 1.25.
1851. P. Mint. Extra fine. 1.25.
1852. O. Mint. Very good. 2.50.
1864. Brilliant proof. 1.50.
1877. S. and C.C. Uncir'd. Pair. 1.50.
1877 to 1881, 1883, 1885, 1888. Brilliant proofs. 8 pcs. Lot. 7.00.
1877 to 1885. Uncirculated. Brilliant mint lustre. 9 pcs. Lot. 6.00.

U. S. Quarters.

1796. Good. 2.00.
1796. Fair. Pierced at top. .75.
1804. Very fair. Bold date. 2.00.
1805. Good. .60.
1806. Very good. .60.
1806 over '05. Very good. .75.
1807. Good. .60.
1815. Good. .50.
1818. Not much circulated. 1.00.
1819. Very good. .40.
1820. Nearly fine. Bold. 50.
1821. Almost uncirculated. 1.25.
1822. Good. .50.
1824. Good. 1.25.
1825. Almost uncirculated. 1.00.
1859, 1860, 1861. Brilliant proof. Each. .65.
1863, 1865. Brilliant proof. Each. .75.
1864. Brilliant proof. 1.25.
1866, 1868, 1872, 1874 (with arrows), 1877, 1878, 1880 to 1883, 1885, 1886, 1889,
    1890. Brilliant proofs. 14 pcs. Lot. 8.50.
1876 to 1886. Uncir'd, mostly semi-proof, one brilliant proof. 11 pcs. 4.00.
U. S. Twenty Cents. 1875. Dull proof. .50.
1876. Uncirculated. .35.

U. S. Dimes.

1796. Good, but head worn, rest bold. 1.50.
1796. Poor, but "Liberty" head and date plain. .75.
1798. Good for date, date bold. 3.50.
1798 over '97. A few stars weak, otherwise very good. 3.50.
1801. Good. Date bold. 4.00. Poor, date visible. .75.
1802. Fair, bold date; good reverse. 3.00.

1803. Fair, bold date. 2.50.
1803. Cracked die. Very good, pierced at top. 1.50.
1804. Fair, but scratched on head, date plain. 7.50.
1805. Very fair. .35. Fair, date plain. .25.
1807. Good. .75. Fair, date plain. .25.
1809. Very fair. .75.
1811. Good. .75. Good, but pierced. .35.

1814. Large 8. Fine. .40.
1820, 1821. Almost fine. Each. .25.
1822. Very fair, date good, but light nicks on obverse. 1.25.
1827. Quite fine. .50.
1828. Large date. Very good or fine, bold. 1.25.
1829. Quite fine. Semi-proof surface. .50.
1831. About uncirculated. .50.
1846. Good. .75.
1860. *With stars.* Good. .35.
1859, 1860, 1861, 1862. Br. proof. Lot. 1.50.
1863. Brilliant proof. .75.
1864. Brilliant proof. 1.00.
1866, 1872, 1873 (with and without arrows), 1874 to 1884, 1886, 1889. Brilliant
    proofs. 17 pcs. 5.00.

U. S. Half Dimes.

1794. Stars to right weak, rest of obverse good, date bold; reverse shows small
    button mark on eagle. 2.50. Very good, small hole above head. 1.50.
    Another good or very good, pierced through lower part of head, above
    date. 1.00.
1795. Very good. 1.25.
1796. Good for date. 2.00. Poor, pierced, date visible. .50.
1797. Good. 2.00. Fair, date bold. 1.25. Poor, 97 of date plain. .50. Stars
    to left weak, otherwise very good, pierced. 1.00. Barely fair, 97 of date
    bold, pierced. .35.
1800. Good. .75. Fair, plain date. .50. Quite fine, but plugged. 1.00.
1801. Stars weak, otherwise good, date bold. 1.50. Fair, bold date. 1.00.
    Very fair, pierced, bold date. .65.
1803. Fair, good date. 1.50. Good, pierced at top. .75.
1805. Very fair or good, plain date. 6.00. Good, pierced at top. 3.00.
1863. Brilliant proof. .75.
1859, 1860, 1866, 1867, 1869, 1870, 1871, 1873. Brilliant proofs. 8 pcs. 2.00.

U. S. Minor Coinage.

1867. Minor proof set. 1, 2, 3, 5 cts. 5 cts. uncir'd. .60.
1869. Minor proof set. 1, 2, 3, 5 cts. Cent uncirculated. .65.
1872. 1, 3, 5 cts. Proof. .45.

1873. Minor proof set. 1, 2, 3, 5 cts. 1.75.
1866, 1869 to 1872, 1876, 1878 to 1881, 1883 (3 var's), 1884 to 1886. Five cents.
    Brilliant proofs. 16 pcs. 4.00.
1878. Five cents. Proof. .35.
1872, 1881, 1883, 1884. Three cents. Proof. Lot, .60.
1866. Two cents. Brilliant proof. .40.
1871. Two cents. Brilliant proof. .40.
1856. Nickel cent. Very good. 3.50.
1861. Nickel cent. Brilliant proof. .75.

U. S. Cents.

1793. Chain. Obverse eroded rough, date plain; rev., fine. 3.50.
1793. Wreath. Very fair or good, but rough surface on both sides. 2.50.
1793. Wreath. Broad leaves. Fair. 2.00.
1793. Liberty head and leaves (broad) plain. Date faintly visible. Copper plug
    through head. .50.
1793. Wreath. Lettered edge. Good. Light pin scratches. 3.50.
1793. Liberty cap. Good. 5.00.
1793. Liberty cap. Barely fair. Date visible. 2.00.
1794. Maris No. 3. "Sans Milling." Fine. Brown. 2.00.
1794. Maris No. 7. "Crooked 7." Fair. .25.
1794. Maris No. 9. "Crooked 7." Good, but small wheel punched on head. .25.
1794. Maris No. 10. "Pyramidal Head." Very fair, screw punch on head. .25.
1794. Maris No. 11. "Many Haired." Very good. .75.
1794. Maris No. 12. "Scarred Head." Good. .50.
1794. Maris No. 13. "Standless 4." Good. Light brown. .75.
1794. Maris No. 14. "Abrupt Hair." Very good. Light brown. 1.00.
1794. Maris No. 15. "Separated Date." Fair. .25.
1794. Maris No. 16. " Separated Date." Fair. .25.
1794. Maris No. 17. "The Ornate." Fine, but three light pin scratches on ob-
    verse. .75.
1794. Maris No. 20. "Fallen 4." Very good. 1.00.
1794. Maris No. 21. "Short Bust." Very good. Brown. .75.
1794. Maris No. 24. "The Patagonian." Fair. .25.
1794. Maris No. 25. "The Ornate." Very good. Olive. 1.25.
1794. Maris No. 26. "Amiable Face." Nearly fine. Steel color. 1.25.
1794. Maris No. 28. " Large Planchet." Very good. Light brown. 1.00.
1794. Maris No. 29. "Marred Field." Nearly fine. Steel color. 1.50.
1794. Maris No. 32. "Shielded Hair." Nearly fine. Brown. 1.50.
1794. Maris No. 36. "The Plicæ." Very fair. .50.
1794. Maris No. 37. "The Plicæ." Nearly fine. Brown. 1.25.
1794. Maris No. 38. "Roman Plicæ." Very good. 1.00.
1794. Maris No. 39. "1795 Head." Quite fine, but rough on reverse. 1.50.
1794. Maris No. 40. "Many Haired." Good. 1.00.
1794. Maris No. 42. "Trephined Head." Fine. Brown. 2.00.
1794. Maris No. 50. Good. 1.00.
1794. Maris No. 52. Scarcely fair, but rare. .35.

1795.   Lettered edge.   Fine, clean, brown color.   3.50.
1795.   Lettered edge.   Good, but rough surface.   1.00.
1795.   Thin.   Very good.   .75.
1796.   Liberty cap.   Very good.   1.25.
1796.   Fillet head.   Very good, bold.   1.50.
1796.   Liherty.   Fair.   .40.
1797.   Fine.   Brown.   1.00.
1797.   No stems to wreath.   Good.   .40.
1798.   Fine or very fine.   1.00.
1799.   Obverse is scarcely fair.   Date worn at bottom, but nearly all of last 9 shows.
         5.00.
1800.   Perfect date.   Fine.   Brown.   1.50.
1800 over '99.   Quite fine, brown color, slight corrosion on reverse.   1.50.
1801.   Nearly fine.   Brown.   1 00.
1801.   1–000 variety.   Very good.   '50.
1801.   1–000 and Hnited variety.   Good.   .50.
1802.   Extremely fine.   Steel color.   1.00.
1802.   No stems to wreath.   Very good.   .35.
1803.   Extremely fine.   Steel color.   1.00.
1803.   1–100 over 1–000.   Fine.   Brown.   Rare.   1.50.
1804.   About good but a little battered.   4.00.   Scarcely fair but date shows.   2.50.
1805.   Fine.   Brown.   2.00.
1806.   Fine.   Brown.   2.00.
1807.   Perfect date.   Quite fine.   Brown.   1.50.
1807 over '06.   Fine.   1.00.
1808.   Fine and bold.   Steel color.   2.00.
1808.   12 stars.   Good, dark.   .50.
1809.   Good.   1.50.
1810 over '09.   Fine.   Brown.   1.25.
1810.   Nearly fine.   Steel color.   .75.
1811 over '10.   Very good, bold.   2.00.
1811.   Good.   1.25.
1812.   Large date.   Almost uncirculated.   Glossy steel color.   2.50.
1813.   Fine.   Brown.   1.25.
1814.   Plain 4.   Nearly fine.   Brown.   .35.
1816.   Perfect die.   Quite fine.   Light olive.   .50.
1817.   Uncirculated.   Sharp.   Glossy brown.   1.25.
1817.   Fifteen stars.   Fine.   Brown.   1.00.
1818.   Uncirculated.   Bright red.   .75.
1818.   Perfect die.   Very fine.   Reddish.   .35.
1819.   Uncirculated.   Bright red.   1.25.
1819.   Stars close to date.   Very good.   Brown.   Rare.   .35.
1820.   Uncirculated.   Bright red.   1.00.   Another.   Clean, brown color.   .75.
1821.   Very good.   Bold.   .50.
1822.   Fine.   Orange color.   1.00.
1823 over '22.   Very good.   .50.
1824.   Fine.   Brown.   1.00.
1825.   Fine.   Light olive.   1.00.
1826.   Very fine.   Purple color.   1.50.
1827.   Fine.   Purple.   .50.
1828.   Fine.   Brown.   .50.
1829.   *Very* good.   Brown.   .50.
1830.   Very fine.   Light brown.   .75.
1831.   Very fine.   Light olive.   .75.
1832.   Fine and bold.   Light color.   .75.
1833.   Fine.   Light olive.   .50.
1834.   Very fine.   Brown.   .50.
1834.   Large date.   Fine.   Brown.   .50.

1835.   Fine.   Light brown.   .50.
1836.   Very fine.   Light olive.   1.00.
1837.   Plain hair string.   Uncirculated.   Olive and partiy bright.   1.50.
1837.   Beaded hair string.   Very fine.   Olive.   .50.
1838.   Barely circulated.   Light brown.   .50.
1839 over '36.   Very fair.   "W. Fay" stamped on head.   1.00.
1839.   Head of 1838.   Very fine.   Brown.   1.25.
1839.   Booby Head.   Very fine.   Brown.   1.00.
1839.   Silly Head.   Fine.   Brown.   .75.
1839.   Head of 1840.   Fine.   Brown.   .75.
1840.   Large date.   Very fine, light brown.   .50.
1840.   Small date.   Fine, brown.   .35.
1841.   Very fine, light olive.   .50.
1842.   Large date.   Very fine, olive.   .50.
1842.   Small date.   Fine, brown.   .35.
1843.   Uncirculated.   Light olive.   2.00.
1844.   Scarcely circulated, beautiful light olive.   6 nicks on reverse milling, not
          visible on obverse.   .50.
1845.   Very fine, purple.   .40.
1846.   Dutch 6.   Very fine, light olive.   .40.
1847.   Barely touched, light olive.   .40.
1848.   Very fine, light olive.   .35.
1849.   About uncirculated.   Brown.   .75.
1850, 1851, 1852, 1853, 1854, 1855, 1856.   Uncirculated, light olive.   Each.   .25.
1857.   Large date,   Uncirculated with traces of brightness.   .50.
1857.   Small date.   Very fine, light brown.   .35.

U. S. Half Cents.

1793.   Fair.   1.25.
1794.   Good.   .60.
1795.   Thin.   Very fair.   .50.
1797.   Fair, good date.   .40.
1802.   Good.   Nick on edge.   1.25.
1811.   Fair.   .40.
1854.   Uncirculated.   Brilliant red.   .40.
1855.   Uncirculated.   Brilliant red.   .30.
1857.   Uncirculated.   Brilliant red.   .30.

Washington Coins.

1783.   "Unity States" Cent.   Good.   .25.
1783.   "United States" Cent.   Good.   .40.
Double-head Cent.   Good.   .50.
1791.   Cent.   Large Eagle.   Very fair.   1.50.   Same, barely fair but good head
          and nearly everything else shows.   .75.
1793.   Halfpenny.   Obverse good; rev., shows "halfpenny" and date plain.
          Rest weak.   .75.
Washington Button.   "G. W." Above, "Long live the President."   Twice pierced.
          1.00.
Washington Button.   Eagle.   "March the fourth 1789 Memorable Era."   Good.
          2.00.

American Colonials.

1783. Chalmers Annapolis shilling. The very rare variety with a long worm. Extremely fine, but a very small hole has been plugged. 7.50.

1783. Chalmers Annapolis threepence. Very fine but small plug. 5.00.

Maryland. Lord Baltimore shilling. The head on obverse is fair, field a little scratched and slightly bruised at bottom, legend good. Reverse very good, slightly bruised at top. 15.00.

Maryland. Lord Baltimore 4 pence or groat. Fine. Minute hole in field. 10.00.

1722. Rosa Americana Twopence. Scarcely fair, but head, rose, date and part of legends plain. .50.

1722. Rosa Americana Penny. Good. .50.

1722. Rosa Americana Halfpenny. Fair. 25.

1723. Rosa Americana Penny. Good. .65. Very fair. .40.

1787. "Mind your business" Cent. Very good. .25. Very fair. .15.

1787. Nova Eborac. Good. .75.

1787. New York Cent. Arms of New York. "Excelsior" below; rev., eagle. Very good but partly pierced, and 1 of date removed. Rare. 12.50.

1783, 1785. Nova Constellatio. Very good. Each .35.

1785. Vermont Res Publica. Date weak, otherwise very good, light brown color. 1.00.

1786. Vermontensium. Very fair. .50.

1788. Vermon Auctori. Very good. .35.

1773. Virginia. Very good. .25.

1787. Massachusetts Cent. Horned Eagle. Very fair. .40.

1788. Mass. Cent. Good. .35.

——. Mass. Half Cent. Very fair, but date gone. .50.

1781. North American Token. Good. .20.

1767. Louisiana Cent. R. F. Good. .60.

1787. Immunis Columbia. Liberty with scales seated on globe. Fair. 2.50.

Mark Newby Farthing. St. Patrick and the snakes. Fair. .50.

New Jersey. Horse head to left. Fair. .75. Another, good but pierced. .75.

New Jersey. "Pluribs" variety. Obverse fair, rev. good. .40.

1787. New Jersey. Large Planchet. Very good. .25.

1794. Talbot, Allum and Lee. Cent. Good. .35.

1721. Louisiana Cent. Very fair. .50.
1787. Connecticut Cent. Good. .20.
1786. Connecticut Cent. Curious double strike with two dates. Very good. .40.
1760. Voce Populi. Very good. .40.

U. S. Patterns.

1792. Martha Washington Half Disme. Good but nicked. 2.50.
1850. Three cents. Liberty Cap in rays. Silver proof. 3.00.
1853. Cent. Nickel pattern. Uncirculated. Pierced at top. .20.
1854. Cent. Liberty head. Proof, but a few trifling light scratches in field. .75.
1855. Cent. Flying eagle. Very fine. Light nicks on edge. .50.
1858. Cent. Nickel. *Small legend.* Uncirculated. .25.
1858. Cent. Indian head. Laurel wreath. Nickel proof. .75.
1859. Half Dollars. Liberty head with reverses "Half Dollar" and "50 Cents"
—also, Liberty seated. Proofs. 3 pcs. Lot. 4.00.
1863. Three Cents. Obverse same as old cent. Copper proof. 2.00.
1863. Two Cents. Brilliant proof. 1.50.
1863. Copper Cent. Thin. Brilliant proof. .75.
1867. Five Cents. Longacre's design. Indian Queen. Aluminum proof. 1.25.
1870. Barber Dollar. Copper proof. 2.50.
1879. Silver Metric and Goloid Dollars. Proof. Pair, 4.00.

Fractional Currency.

(All new and clean.)

50, 25, 10, 5 Cents. Perforated edges. 5.00.
50, 25, 10, 5 Cents. Plain edges. 2.00.
50, 25, 10, 5 Cents. Washington in gilt ring. 2.50.
50, 25, 10, 5 Cents. Washington in gilt ring. Paper that will split. 5.00.
50 Cents. Justice. Red back. Auto. sign. of Colby and Spinner. 3.00.
50 Cents. Justice. Red back. No letters on rev. 2.50.
50 Cents. Justice. Red back. Letters on rev. Slightly used. 1.50.
50 Cents. Justice. Green back. 2.00.
50 Cents. Spinner. Red back. Auto. sign. of Allison and Spinner. 5.00.
50 Cents. Spinner. Red back. Auto. sign. of Colby and Spinner. 3.00.
50 Cents. Spinner. Red back. 2.25.
50 Cents. Spinner. Green back. "50" at ends. 1.50.
50 Cents. Spinner. Green back. "50" in centre. 1.75.
25 Cents. Fessenden. Red back. 1.50. Green back. .50.
25 Cents. Fessenden. Green back. Coarse fiber paper, gilt letters on reverse.
Heavy but not solid disc. 5.00.
25 Cents. Fessenden. Green back. Coarse fiber paper. Solid discs. 20.00.
15 Cents. Grant and Sherman. Red and green backs. Broad margins. Auto. sign.
of Allison and Spinner. Pair 20.00.
15 Cents. Grant and Sherman. Auto. sign. of Jeffries and Spinner. Obverse
only. 2.50.
15 Cents. Grant and Sherman. Red back. Auto. sign. of Allison and Spinner. 8.00.
10 Cents. Washington. Red back. Auto. sign. of Jeffries and Spinner. 2.00.
10 Cents. Washington. Red back. Auto. sign. of Colby and Spinner. 1.50.
10 Cents. Washington. Red back. 1.00. Green back. .35.
5 Cents. Clark. Red back. .75. Green back. .35.
3 Cents. Washington. .40. Dark curtain. .75.

50 Cents.   Lincoln.   1.50.
50 Cents.   Stanton.   .85.
25 Cents.   Washington.   .50.
15 Cents.   Liberty.   .60.
10 Cents.   Liberty.   .35.
50 Cents.   Dexter.   .75.
10 Cents.   Merideth.   Green seal.   .50.   Red seal.   .25.
Shield of Fractional Currency as issued by U. S.   Contains two Grant and Sherman
    15 cent notes, etc.   Framed.   20.00.

The following are all signed in autograph on the reverse.

50 Cents.   Crawford.   Auto. sign. of " Jno. C. New."   5.00.
50 Cents.   Crawford.   Auto. sign. of " B. K. Bruce, Register U. S. Treasury."
    5.00.
50 Cents.   Crawford.   Auto. sign. of " Jas. Gilfillan, Treasurer U. S."   5 00.
50 Cents.   Crawford.   Auto. sign. of " A. U. Wyman, Treasurer U. S."   5.00.
25 Cents.   Walker.   Auto. sign. of " B. K. Bruce, Register U. S. Treasury."   5.00.
25 Cents.   Walker.   Auto. sign. of " Jas. Gilfillan, Treasurer U. S."   5.00.
25 Cents.   Walker.   Auto. sign. of " A. U. Wyman, Treasurer U. S."   5.00.
10 Cents.   Merideth.   Auto. sign. of " Jas. Gilfillan, Treasurer U. S."   5.00.
10 Cents.   Merideth.   Auto. sign. of " A. U. Wyman, Treasurer U. S."   5.00.
 5 Cents.   Clark.   Red and green backs. Both with auto. sign. of Clark on reverse.
    Pair 10.00.

The following are all extremely rare.

50 Cents.   2nd issue.   No gilt ring around Washington.   Coarse fiber paper.   Plain
    reverse.   7.50.
50 Cents.   2nd issue.   The obverse has the large gilt outline 50 and gilt figures in
    corners usually found on the reverse, otherwise plain.   The reverse is the
    usual design, but with the gilt ring usually found on the obverse around the
    50, and lacking the designs which on this note are on the obverse.   Coarse
    fiber paper.   7.50.
50 Cents.   2nd issue.   Obverse plain except a gilt ring; reverse as usual.   Coarse
    fiber paper.   7.50.
10 Cents.   2nd issue.   Obverse plain except a gilt ring; reverse as usual.   Coarse
    fiber paper.   7.50.
 5 Cents.   2nd issue.   Obverse plain; reverse lacks the outlined figure and is differ-
    ently shaded from the regular note, the eagle and stars on border being light
    where dark on the usual note and *vice versa*.   The color is a light gold-
    brown.   *Unique.*   15.00.

Hard Times Tokens.

Negress in chains.   " Am I not a woman and a sister?"   Very good.   .25.
Steer.   " A friend to the Constitution."   Rev., ship, " Agriculture and Commerce."
    Very good.   .75.
Same.   Rev., W. Gibbs' card.   Very fair or good.   .50.
Donkey.   Rev., turtle.   Uncirculated.   Bright red.   .25.
Loco Foco.   Fine.   .50.
Head of Jackson; rev., hog running.   Uncirculated.   Partly bright.   .40.
Ship; rev., wrecked ship.   Uncirculated.   Bright red.   .75.
1837.   Liberty head.   13 stars.   No. 27.   Very good.   1.00.
1837.   Liberty head.   15 stars (a small star on each side of date).   No. 28.   Very
    good.   1.00.
1837.   " United " head, large date.   No. 29.   Good.   1.00.

Foreign Crowns.

Austria.   1558.   Ferdinand I.   Very good.   2.50.
1569.   Maxmilian II.   Very good.   2.50.
1603.   Rudolph II.   Fine.   2.50.

1620. Ferdinand II. Fine. 2.25.
1630. Ferdinand II. Very good. 2.00.
1639. Ferdinand IV. Broad Crown. Fine. 2.50.
1657. Ferdinand III. Very good. 2.00.
1661. Leopold. Very good. 2.00.
Brunswick. 1624. Christian. Broad ruff around neck. Very good. 2.00.
1638. Frederick. Gothic inscriptions. Very good. 2.25.
Basle. *Broad Double Crown.* No date, but about 1600. *View of the City.* Very
     good. 5.00.
Gotha. 1567. Siege crown. Crossed swords. Very good. 2.50.
Guilders. 1616. Good. 1.75.
Guilders. 1650. Good. 1.50.
Hungary. 1621. Very good, but corroded on reverse. 1.50.
Nurnberg. 1626. Ferdinand II. Good, but a little corroded. 1.50.
1680. View of the city. Fine. 1.75.
1763. View of the city. Very good. 1.50.
Parma. 1628. Odorado Farnese. Rev., St. Anthony with ensign. Fine. 2.50.
Presburg. 1725. Wolfgang. Uncirculated. 1.75.
Salzburg. 1619. Marcus Sitticus. Very good. 2.50.
Schaffhausen. 1621. Ram springing from temple door. Very good. 2.00.
Saxony. 1595. Busts of 3 dukes. Very good. 2.50.
1624. John Philip. Bust; rev., procession of 3 dukes. Very good. 2.50.
1650. John George. Very good. 2.50.

War Medals.

War Medals. West Virginia. 1861–1865. Abused and corroded. Scarce.
     Bronze. Size 24. .35.
Crimea. 1854. No bar or ribbon, good, silver, size 24. 1.50.
India. 1857–58. Same; rev., Una and lion. No bar or ribbon. Very fine. Sil-
     ver. Size 23. 2.25.
Afghanistan. 1878–80. Rev., elephant artillery. Plain bar. Semi-proof. Silver.
     Size 24. 3.00.
France. Napoleon III. Expedition to China. 1860. Head, rev., names of
     battles. Silver. Size 20. Dull proof. 1.50.

Ancient and Foreign Gold.

Ancient Scythian gold coin. Ardokro. King at fire altar; rev., king seated on
     throne. Extremely fine and very rare. Size 14. 15.00.
Audh, India. Gold Mohur. Obverse, two mermaids holding flags and supporting
     a crown. Extremely fine. 15.00.
Bavaria. Charles Theodore. 1780. Bust; rev., river god, and view of Munich.
     Ducat struck from gold from the river Isar. Proof. 5.00.
Turkey. Gold. Proof. Size 14. 2.00.
Transylvania. 1657. George Rakoczi II. Ducat. Uncirculated. 6.00.
Mexico. ⅛ Doubloon. 1869. Proof surface. 2.75.
Spain. 1786. Chas. IV. Dollar size. Fine. 1.50.
Persia. Darius I. B. C. 521. Gold Daric. King with bow kneeling. Very
     fine. 25.00.
Roman. (457) Leo I. Rev., Victory holding a cross. Solidus. Very good. 5.00.
(474) Zeno. Rev., Victory holding a cross. Solidus. Very good. 5.00.
(630) Heraclius and son. Rev., cross on pedestal. Solidus. Very fine. 6.00.

Oriental Silver.

Anam. Taele or Dragon Dollar. Grinning human-faced dragon's head above sun;
     rev., 4 characters around sun. Uncirculated. Rare. 5.00.
Anam. Silver duk. Dragons. Extremely fine. 2.00.
Oudh, India. Wadschid Ali. 1850. ⅛ rupee. Two mermaids. Very fine. 1.50.
Bidsnagur, India. Half Fanam. Dancing deity. Very fine. 1.00.

Madras. Quarter Pagoda. Tower surrounded by stars; rev., god Vishnu in circle of dots. Fine. 1.50.

Assam. Octagonal Rupee. Very fine. Rare. 2.00.

Burmah. Rupee, ¼ and ⅛. Peacock with spread tail. Very fine. Set for 4.00.

Japan. Itzebue. Uncirculated. .75.

Japan. ¼ Itzebue. Uncirculated. .35.

Siam. Bullet money. Tical. Very fine. 1.25.

Siam. Bullet money. ¼ and ⅛ Tical. Very fine. Each .75.

Persia. ¼ Kran. Sun-lion with sword (dime size). Uncirculated. .50.

Japan. Oblong silver coin, 3½ x 1⅜ in. The obverse is covered with characters, also two circular stamps with characters near each end. Fine and rare. Weight 4½ oz. Av. 10.00.

Japan. Oblong, one pear shaped, silver dumps, each stamped with characters. They range in size from a pea to ¾ oz. I do not think two sizes are alike. Fine lot. 13 pieces. 12.50.

Siam. Circulars coin with elephant and royal umbrellas. 2, 1, ½, ¼, ⅛ Tical. Uncirculated. 6.00.

Corea. 1 and 2 Stubs (size 14 and 18.) Coined as indemnity money to China. Obverse with porcelain centre; rev., four characters. Very curious and rare. Uncirculated. Pair for 5.00.

Siam. Bullet money. 4, 2, 1, ½, ¼, ⅛, $\frac{1}{32}$ Tical. Full set except $\frac{1}{16}$ Tical. Fine and desirable. 10.00.

Anam. Loaf-shaped, or more properly something like a cap with two visors. Bears three counter-stamps, two of which are from dies, one native characters— the other English, and the third being the autograph of some native merchant. Remarkable as to weight, which is 12 oz. Av. Fine and desirable. 25.00.

Anam. Coin similar to last, but outside and edges smoothly polished, die stamp on bottom, and four characters on top. 5.00.

Cambodia. Silver coins. Obverses, odd bird and bird idol. Very fine. Size 8 Each, .50.

Saurashtran, Hindu. Curious figure somewhat resembling a pelican. Size 10. Fine. 1.50.

India. Small dump with idol. Fine. .50.

Morocco. 1286. Size 12. Fine. .50.

Zanzibar. 1299. Size 10. Uncirculated. Rare. .75.

Foreign Silver.

New Grenada. 1849. Head of Liberty. Pattern Peso by Wyon. 4 designs. *Beautiful proofs.* Lot for 10.00.

Venezuela. Head of Bolivar. ½, ¼, $\frac{1}{10}$, $\frac{1}{20}$ Peso. *Beautiful proof set of patterns* by Barre. Rare. Lot for 7.50.

Sweden. 1871. Chas. XV. 4 R. M., 2 R. M., 50, 25, 10 Ore. *Beautiful proofs.* Set for 5.00.

Mexico. 1758. Ferd. VI. Dollar. G. R. (Georgius Rex) die-counterstamped on each side for use in England. Fonrobert 6336. Fine. Rare. 5.00.

Central America. Sun rising behind mountain peaks. But little circulated. 1.25.

Republic of Columbia. Indian head and pomegranate. 2, 8 Reals. Very good. Pair. 1.75.

U. S. of Colombia. 1868. Half Dollar. Very fine. 1.00.

Bolivia. 1845. Llamas under tree. Dollar. Uncirculated. Mint lustre. 2.50.

Peru. 1833. Liberty standing. Dollar. Barely circulated. Mint lustre. 2.00.

Peru. 1862, 1863, 1864. Callao and Lima. Indian, Liberty in chariot, steamboat. Tokens. ¼ dollar size. Semi-proof. 3 pieces. Lot. 2.50.

Chili. 1874. Dollar. Condor. Barely circulated. 1.50.

Chili. Mining Dollar. Plain planchet with star and 1 P. in sunken counterstamp. Fine. 2.00.

La Plata. 1, 2, 4, 8 Reals (Dollar). Sun in Rays. Very fine. Lot. 3.00.

Cordoba. (Argentine Conf.) Dollar. Fort surrounded by seven flags. Very fine. Rare. 5.00.

Uruguay. 1877. 50, 20, 10 Centavos. Mint lustre. Lot for 1.25.

Venezuela. 1858. Half Dollar. Fine. 1.00.

Ecuador. 1855. Half Dollar. Fine. 1.00.

Caracas. 1811. 2 Reals. Very fine. Rude. .40.

France. Louis XIIII. 1652. Crown. Young head. Very fine. 2.50.

Louis XIIII. 1690. Crown. Old head. Fine. 2.00.

Louis XV. 1728. Crown. Very good. 1.50.

Republic. 1852. Louis Napoleon Bonaparte. 50c, 1, 5 Francs. Uncirculated. Mint bloom. 1.75.

Bavaria. Maximilian II. 1853. ½, 1, 2 Gulden, 1 Thaler. Uncirculated. Mint bloom. Lot 2.50.

Papal States. Pius IX. 1869. ½, 1, 2 Lire. Proof surface. Lot 1.15.

Spain. Ferd. VI. 1755. Mexico mint. Dollar. Crowned globes between pillars. A splendid specimen in nearly brilliant proof condition. 4.00.

Luzern, Switzerland. 1814. Broad Crown. Uncirculated. 2.50.

Neapolitan Republic. Liberty standing. Year 7. Fine. 2.50.

Russia. 1860. Rouble. Proof. 1.00.

Sicily. 1855. Ferd. II. Crown. Uncirculated. 1.25.

Straits Settlements. 10 Cents. Extremely fine. .25.

Sandwich Islands. Kalakaua I. Dime. Brilliant proof. .50.

Japan. Dragon. Yen, 50, 20, 10, 5 sen. Uncirculated. Lot 2.50.

Ceylon. 1821. Elephant. Rix dollar. Uncirculated. 2.00.

Bolivia. 1868. Pattern set. 5, 10, 20 Centavos, 1 Boliviano. State Arms. Rev., Condor standing. Silver proofs. 7.50.

Bolivia. 1884. 5, 10, 20, 50 Centavos, 1 Boliviano. State Arms. Brilliant proofs. 7.50.

Sierra Leone. 1791. Dollar. Lion. Fine. 2.50.

Sierra Leone. 1791. Dime. Lion. Fine. .50.

Ecuador. Sucre (Dollar) and ⅕ Sucre. Uncirculated. Mint lustre. Pair 2.00.

Sandwich Islands. 1883. Kalakaua I. Dollars, ½, ¼, 1/10. Uncirculated. Mint lustre. Set 3.50.

Hayti. 1881. Gourde (Dollar), 20, 10 cts. Beautiful design. Brilliant mint lustre. Set 2.50.

Hong Kong. Dollar and ½ Dollar. Barely circulated. Pair 2.00.

China. Mexican Dollar with Chinese chop-mark. 1.25.

Switzerland. 1814. Canton Soloth'n. Crown. Fine. 2.00.

Switzerland. 1851. 5 Francs. Mint bloom. 1.35.

New Grenada. 1847. 2, 8 Reals. Very fine. Scarce. Pair 1.50.

Bolivia. 1884. Dime. Br. Proof. .50.

Sardinia. 1859. Victor Emmanuel. 5 Lire. Brilliant mint lustre. 1.50.

Papal States. 1836. Gregory XVI. Scudo. Uncir'd. 1.50.

Austria. 1780. Maria Theresa. Levant Crown. Uncir'd. 1.50.

Brunswick. 1670, etc. Wild man. 4, 6, 12, 24 Gros. Very fine. Lot 2.50.

Mexico. 1866. Maxmilian. Dollar and half. Barely circulated. Pair 2.50.

1841. Bolivia. Bolivar. Llamas under tree. Dollar. Barely cir'd. 1.50.

1837. South Peru. Dollar. Human faced sun: rev., volcano, ship, fort, etc. Barely circulated. 1.50.

1842. Peru. Dollar. Liberty with spear and shield. Very fine. Mint lustre. 1.50.

1867. Peru. Dollar. Seated Liberty. Uncirculated. 1.25.

1877. Chili. Dollar. Condor. Uncirculated. 1.50.

1726. France. Louis XV. Crown. Good. 1.25.

Japan. Dollar. Dragon and sun. Uncirculated. 1.50.

Japan. 50 Sen. Dragon. Uncirculated. .75.

1821. Spain. Ferd. VII. Dollar. About uncirculated. 1.25,

1817. Spain. Ferd. VII. Dollar. Counterstamped for Brazil. Extremely fine. 1.25.

Tranquebar. Dump with idol. Very fine. .65.

France. Napoleon III. 1852. ½, 1 fr. Uncirculated. 2 pcs. Lot. .50.

Mexico. 1808. Aug. 15. Arms crowned. Proclamation medal. Size 18. Extremely fine. 1.25.

Mexico. 1821. Oct. 27. Secretary bird on cactus. Proclamation of Independence medal. Br. proof. Size 22. 1.50.

Mexico. 1822. July 21. Same design. Inauguration medal of Augustin. Size 22. Barely touched proof. 1.25.

Another. All but as fine. 1.00.

San Luis Potosi. Indian queen seated. Medal for its patriots. Size 19. About uncirculated. 1.50.

India. Old rupee, curious die-counterstamp of man on horseback. Very fine. 2.00.

Persia. Size 11. Brilliant. Uncirculated. .50.

Assam. Octagonal rupee, curious dragon at bottom, extremely fine. 2.00.

Assam. Octagonal ¼, ½, 1 rupee, very fine. 3 pcs. Lot. 3.00.

Triangular sections of Spanish coins, three counter-stamped with C (Cayenne?), one with 3. Fine. 4 pcs. Lot. 3.50.

Kempten. Bust of the Bishop. Bracteates. Size 14. Uncirculated. 10 pcs. Lot 2.50.

Lille. Marshal's batons crowned, rev., mailed arm with sword. "Non sine numine," necessity money, very fine, size 19. 1.50.

1648. Deventer. Diamond-shaped siege piece. Bust; rev., flower pot. Fine. 1.50.

France. Louis XV. 1721. Bust with long curls. View of islands, "Guadalupa insula muneta. Philippo regente." Brilliant proof. Size 26. 2.50.

Scene of Manger, odd design, very fine. Size 22. 1.00.

Foreign silver, from 10 to 25 cents size. Uruguay, India, Hayti, Caracas, a square coin, another with a ram, etc. Very desirable. Many uncirculated. No duplicates. 25 pcs. Lot. 4.00.

Foreign silver. Another lot, 10 to 25 cent size. Nicaragua, Turkey, Japan, mediæval, English 1679, Hanover, etc. As choice as last lot, many uncirculated. No duplicates. 25 pcs. Lot. 4.00.

France. Henry III. Testoons. 1576, 1577, 1587. Good to fine. 4 pcs. Lot. 2.00.

Turkey. Cup-shaped coins. Size 23 (2), 18. Fine but pierced. 3 pcs. Lot. 1.00.

Venice. 1734, etc. Kneeling saints, winged lion. Largest (size 20), fine, other (size 13) good, one pierced. 2 pcs. Pair. 1.00.

Small bracteates. 25 pcs. Lot. 1.00.

Zacatecas. 1811. Provisional dollar. Very fair. 2.00.

Zacatecas. Ferd. VII. Provisional 2 reals. Very fair. .50.

Zacatecas. Mountain with cross. 2 reals. Very fair. .75.

Mexico. 1812. Vargas dollar. Fair (never found better). 1.25.

Mexico. 1822. Augustine dollar. Nearly uncirculated. Lustre. 1.75.
Central America. Sun rising behind mountain peaks. 1, 2 reals. Pair. .50.
Guatemala. 1760. Chas. III. Proclamation 2 reals. Good, but twice pierced.
Rare. .40.
Guatemala. 1808. Ferd. VII. Proclamation 2 reals. Mountain. Very good.
1.50.
Same. 1 real. Good. Pierced. .35.
Guatemala. Sept. 24, 1812. 2 reals. Open book in rays, arms of Guatemala.
Fine. Pierced. .50.
Louis XV. and XVI. Tokens. 1735, 1741, etc. ½, ¼ (3) Crowns. Ship under
full sail, Justice with scales, tree growing, etc. Fine. 4 pcs. 2.50.
Louis XVI. 1793. Crown. Rev., angel inscribing tablet, cock and faces on
sides. Extremely fine. 2.50.
Louis XVI. 1791, 1793. 15, 30 Sols. Angel inscribing tablet. Fine. Pair.
1.00.
Republic. 1793. 6 Livres. Angel inscribing tablet, cock and faces on sides.
Very good. 1.25.
Republic. 1849. 20, 50c., 1, 5 Francs. Uncirculated. Mint bloom. Lot. 1.75.
Republic. 1852. Louis Napoleon Bonaparte. 50c., 1, 5 Francs. Uncirculated.
Mint bloom. 1.75.
Chili. 1877. Dollar. Volcano; rev., pillar surmounted by globe. Barely circu-
lated. Lustre. 2.00.
Prussia. 1871. Siege Thaler. Fine. 1.00.

Silver Coins of Great Britain.

Early British Tetradrachm. Idiotic head; rev., shadowy horseman on colossal
horse. Very fine. 6.00.
Stycae. Rude horse. Copper. Fine. 1.50.
Ethelred II. 978. Head filleted. Rev., small cross in circle. Silver penny. Ex-
tremely fine. 3.00.
Ethelred II. 978. Holding sceptre, large cross on rev. Silver penny. Very
fine. 2.00.
William the Conqueror. 1066. Silver penny. Extremely fine. 3.00. Fine. 2.00.
Good. 1.50.
Henry I. 1100. Silver penny. Very good. 1.50.
Henry II. 1154. Silver penny. Good. 1.00.
John. 1199. Head in triangle; rev., crescent and star. Silver penny. Very fine.
1.50.
Henry III. 1216. Silver penny. Very good. .50.
Edward I. 1272. Silver penny. Fine. .50.
Edward I. 1272. Groat. Good. .75.
Edward II. 1307. Silver penny. Fine. .50.
Edward III. 1327. Half Groat. Fine. .75.
Henry IV. 1399. Groat. Fine. .75.
Henry VI. 1422. Groat. Very fine. 1.00.
Henry VI. 1422. Silver penny. Very fine. .75.
Edward IV. 1461. Half Groat. Very fair. .40.
Henry VII. 1485. Half Groat. Very good. Rare. 1.00.
Henry VIII. 1509. Groat. Side view. Fine. .75.
Henry VIII. 1509. Groat. Front face. Fine. 1.00. Good. .50.
Henry VIII. 1509. Silver penny. Very fine. .75. Very fair. .40.
Edward VI. 1547. Broad Shilling. Very fine. 2.00. Fine. 1.50.
Mary. 1553. Groat. Very fine. 2.00. Good. 1.25.
Mary. 1553. Groat. Bust of Mary. Legend " Philip and Maria." Fine. 2.00.
Philip and Mary. 1553. Broad shilling. Busts facing. Very fine. 5.00.
Elizabeth. 1601. Crown. Very good, fine for this piece. Very rare. 20.00.
Elizabeth. 1558. Shilling. Fine. .75.
Elizabeth. 1561. Sixpence. Fine. .60. Good. .35.

Elizabeth. 1562. Milled Sixpence. Extremely fine. 2.00.
James I. 1603. Half Crown. King on horseback. Very fair. 1.25.
James I. 1603. Shilling. Fine. 1.25. Very good. .75.
James I. 1605. Sixpence. Extremely fine. 1.25. Fine. .75. Good. .50.
Charles I. 1625. Half Crown. King on horseback. Good. 2.00.
Charles I. 1625. Shilling. Fine. .75. Good. .50.
Charles I. 1625. Oromond Crown, Half Crown, Shilling and Sixpence. Good. Set for 20.00.
Commonwealth. 1653. Shilling. Extremely fine. 3.50.
Commonwealth. 1651. Sixpence. Extremely fine. 2.50.
Commonwealth. 1653. Twopence. Fine. 1.00.
Commonwealth. 1653. Penny. Fine. 1.00. Good. .75.
Commonwealth. 1653. Halfpenny. Fine. Rare. 1.50.
Oliver Cromwell. 1658. Crown. A beautiful uncirculated specimen, the crack in the die scarcely showing. 50.00.
Oliver Cromwell. 1658. Crown. Only the barest touch of circulation on most prominent parts of obverse. 30.00. Another, fine. 20.00.
Oliver Cromwell. 1658. Half Crown. Extremely fine. 20.00. Very good. 10.00.
Oliver Cromwell. 1658. Shilling. Barely circulated. 15.00. Fine. 10.00.
Charles II. 1665. Pattern farthing in silver. Uncirculated. 3.50.
Charles II. 1680. Crown. Good. 2.00.
William and Mary. 1689. Half Crown. Rev., shield crowned. Good. 1.00.
William and Mary. 1693. Half Crown. Rev., 4 shields, monogram W M and date in angles. Very good. 1.50.
William III. 1696. Crown. Fine. 2.50.
William III. 1697. Half Crown. Good. 1.00.
Anne. 1707. Crown. Rev., roses and plumes in the angles. Fine. 3.00.
Anne. 1712. Half Crown, Shilling. Sixpence, Fourpence. Good to fine. Lot 2.00.
James III., Old Pretender. 1708. Touch piece. Obv., ship sailing, " Jas. III." etc.; rev., St. Michael and dragon. Extremely fine, has been pierced, but so neatly filled as to be almost invisible. 3.00.
Geo. II. 1758. Shilling. Almost uncirculated. .50.
Geo. III. 1787. Shilling. Uncirculated. .50.
1804. Bank of England. Dollar. Fine. 1.75.
Geo. III. 1818, 1819. Pistrucci Crown. St. George and the dragon. Proof. 7.50.
Scotland. Robert II. 1370. Groat. Very good. 1.50.
James VI. 1594. Thistle Mark. Bust of James; rev., thistle. Fine. 5.00.
James VI. 1601. Thistle Mark. Shield; rev., thistle. Fine. 5.00.
Ireland. 1723. Wood Sixpence. Similar in design to the Wood halfpence, which were rejected in Ireland and then extensively circulated in America. Extremely fine and *excessively rare.* 25.00.

Foreign Coppers.

Where more than one piece is given on a line, the price is for all and not per piece.

Antigua. 1836. Palm tree. Farthing. Fine. .50.
Argentine Confederation. Head of Liberty. 1, 2 Centavos. Uncirculated. Bright red. .50.
Andora. 1873. 10 Centimes. Proof. The only coin of this little republic. .50.
British Honduras. 1885. Cent. Uncirculated. Bright red. .25.

Barbadoes. Penny. Negro head and pineapple. Uncirculated. Light olive. 2.50.
    Fine. .75. Good. .50.
Barbadoes. Penny and Halfpenny. Neptune in car. Also, Penny. Pineapple.
    Set of 3 pcs. Proofs. Handsome. 15.00.
Bermuda. 1793. Penny. Extremely fine. Light olive. .75.
Bahama. Halfpenny. Ship sailing. Uncirculated. Brown. .50.
Bulgaria. 1880. Alex. I. 10 Santum. Bright red. Rare. Proof. .50.
Bulgaria. 1879. Proclamation 10 Santum. Brilliant red proof. .50.
Brazil. 100, 200 Reis. Fine and uncir'd. .50.
Brazil. 80 Reis. Uncirculated. Brilliant red. .50.
Byzantine (Constantinople before the Turkish occupation). Cup-shaped. Fine. 1.00.
    Good. .50.
Congo Free States. 1, 2, 5, 10 Centimes. Round hole in centre. Uncirculated.
    Bright red. Set for .35.
Cambodia. Norodom I. 1860. 5, 10 Centesimos. Beautiful proofs. 1.00.
Cyprus. 1, ½, ¼ Piastre. Uncirculated. Bright red. 1.00.
Ceylon. 1 Stiver. Without date. Thick dump. Fine. .75.
Ceylon. 1802. 2 Stubers. Oblong bar. Very good. 1.50.
Ceylon. 1818. 2 Stubers. Oblong bar. Very good. 1.50.
Ceylon. 1802. 1–48, 1–96, 1–192 R. Elephant. Brilliant proofs. Gold plated
    (issued from Mint that way). 3.00.
Ceylon. 1815. ½, 1, 2 Stivers. Elephant. Very good and fine. 2.00.
Carthagena. Indian under tree. ¼, 2 R. Very good. .75.

Cape of Good Hope. 1889. Penny. Brilliant proof. .50.
Caracas. ¼ R. Very fine. .25.
Canada. Montreal and Lachine Railroad Co. Engine and beaver. Large. Extra
    fine. 3.00. Fine. 2.50. Good. 2.00.
Canada. White's Farthing, Halifax. Very fine. 7.50.
Canada. H. Gagnon & Co. Beaver. Very fine. 1.00.
Canada. A large collection, including a number of scarce pieces. In condition
    from very fair to very fine. Le Roux Nos. 7, 8, 12, 18, 21, 25, 27, 29, 30,
    32, 34, 37, 38, 39, 40, 41, 42, 43, 44, 45, 48, 50, 51, 55, 63, 69, 71, 72, 78,
    80, 82, 83, 90, 91, 93, 95, 96, 97, 99, 101, 104, 105, 118, 119, 127, 129, 135,
    143, 144, 151, 153, 168, 173, 176, 178, 179, 180, 186, 187, 188, 191, 196, 197,
    200, 202, 203, 206, 210, 211, 216, 217, 218, 220, 223, 226, 227, 228.   77 pcs.
    Lot for 7.50.
Caucasus. Native rulers. 1719. Elephant. Bisti. Very good. 1.00.
Dominica. 1848. ¼ R. Very fine. .25.
Dominica. 1877. Centavo. Uncirculated. .25.
Dominica. 1877. 2½ Centavos. Nickel. Proof. .25.
Dutch East Indies. 6 St. 4¾ inches long. VI—St at each end on both sides.
    Very fine. Excessively rare. 15.00.
Dutch East Indies. 4¾ St. Over two inches long. Thick. Monogram of the
    Dutch East India Co. and 4¾ St. on each side. Very fine. Excessively
    rare. 10.00.
England. 1675. Carolus A Carolo. Farthing. Fine. .50. Good. .25.

1680· Charles II. Halfpenny for Ireland. Good. .25.
1686. James II. Halfpenny for Ireland. Good. .25.
1694. William and Mary. Farthing. Fine. .50.
1698. William III. Halfpenny for Ireland. Good. .25.
1714. Anne. Farthing. Bust; rev., Britannia seated, 1714. Uncirculated. Glossy light brown color. 15.00.
Geo. III. 1797. Twopenny. Weight 2 oz. Uncirculated. 2.50. Fine. 1.50. Good. 1.00. Fair. .50.
1796 Geo. III. Penny. Weight 1 oz. Uncirculated. 1.50.
1847. · Victoria. ½ Farthing. Uncirculated. Bright red. .20.
1793· Coventry Halfpenny. Lady Godiva; rev., elephant. Almost uncirculated. Light color. 1.00. Fine. .75. Good. .50.
1794. Similar; rev., clock tower. Fine. .50.
1795. Similar; rev., elephant. Extremely rare. Not in Conder. Very fine. Light brown. 5.00.
English Token. Elephant. "God preserve London." Obverse is from same die as the very rare Carolina cent. Fine. 1.50. Good. 1.00.
Ecuador. 1872. 1, 2 Centavos. Very good. Rare. 1.50.
Ecuador. 1884. ½, 1 Centavos. Nickel. Very rare. Very fine pair. 2.50.
France. Henry III. Double Tournois. Fine. .35.
Guatemala. 1871. Centavo. Mountain peaks. Good. .50.

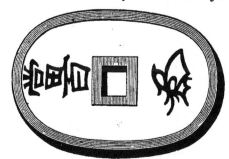

Greece. 1833. Crowned shield. 1, 5, 10 Lepta. Uncir'd. Bright red. 1.00.
Greece. Head. 1, 2, 5, 10 Lepta. Uncirculated. Bright red. 1.00.
Guiana (Spanish). Lion; rev., castle. Very good. Rude. .50.
Georgia. 1717–1724. Nawiz III. Bisti. Peacock. Very good. Rare. 1.50.
Guernsey. 1, 2, 4, 8 Doubles. Fine set. 1.00.
Hungary. 1, 3 Kreutzer. Uncirculated. Bright. .50.
Hong Kong. Cent and Mil. Uncirculated. Bright. .30.
Halifax. Ferry Token. Brilliant red proof. 2.00. Uncirculated. Light olive. 1.00.
Island of Sumatra. Fine. .25.
Ionian Isles. ¼ and ½ Obolo. Very fine and good. .50.
Isle of Man. 1733. Eagle and cradle. This and the following have the three legs joined on reverse. Very good. .50.
1786. George III. Penny. Fine. .50.
1813. Head of Geo. III. Uncirculated. Light olive. 1.50. Nearly as choice. 1.00.
Island of Ceylon. Vidschaya Bahu II. 1186–1187. Same. Massa. Very fine. 1.00.
Bhuvanaika Bahu. 1296–1314. Same. Massa. Very fine. 1.00.
Ireland. Gun Money of James II. A remarkably large collection, containing nearly all the varieties. In condition from fair to about uncirculated; many are very fine, the best a former owner could find out of hundreds examined. Half Crowns. 1689: Jan., Mar., July, Aug., Sep., Dec. 1690: Apr., May (large and small), July. 1690: King on horseback. Shillings. 1689: Jan., Feb., Mar., July, Aug., Aug't, Sep'r, Sep't, 9. Oct, 10, Nov., Dec. 1690: Apr., May, may, June, Sep. Sixpences. 1689: Jan., Feb., June, July, Aug., Sep'r, 7ber, Dec. 37 pieces. 25.00.

Java. ¼ St. Fine. .35.
Jamaica. Penny and Halfpenny. Alligator above shield. Nickel. Very good. .35.
Japan. Tempo. Oblong. (See cut.) Fine. .15.
Liberia. 1833. Negro, tree and ship. Uncirculated. Brown. .50.
Liberia. 1847. Cent. Palm tree. Extremely fine. .50. Good. .25.
Liberia. 1862. Cent and Two Cents. Uncirculated and brilliant proof. Handsome color. 2.50. Another pair, fine. 1.00.
Liberia. 1862. Two Cents. Proof. 1.50. 1.00. Extremely fine. .75.
Malacca. 1250. "Cock of the Walk" (See cut). Very fine. .35.
Magdalen Island. Seal and dried codfish. Fine. 1.50. Good. 1.00. Very fair. .75.
Meysore. Elephant. Thick dump. 5 Cash. Very fine. .50.
Meysore. Lion. Thick dump. 20 Cash. Very fine. .75.
Mexico. Chihuahua. 1860. Liberty seated. ¼ R. Very good. .50.
Chihuahua. 1846. ¼ R. Indian. Fine. .60. Very good. .35.
Jalisco. ¼, ⅛ R. Female with flag. Good. 1.00.
Sinaloa. Head of Liberty. ¼ R. Fine. .50. Good. .25.
Sonora. Female with flag. Cuartilla. Very good. .75.
Zacatecas. Quartilla. Temple and angel. Almost uncirculated. 1.50. Very good. 1.00.
Zacatecas. Octavo. Temple and angel. Very good. 1.00.
Guanaxuati. 1856. Cuartilla. Fine and rare. 1.00.
Mexico. 1864. Centavo of Maxmilian. Fine. 1.00. Good. .50.
Orange Free States. 1888. Penny. Brilliant proof. .35.
Persia. Fath Ali Schah. 1797-1834. 1½ Bisti. Rabbit. Very good. 1.00.
Same ruler. 1½ Bisti. Sun-lion. Fine. 1.00.
Mohammed-Kerim-Khan. 1759-1779. 1½ Bisti. Wedge shaped bar covered on one side with characters. 1½ inches. Very good. 1.00.
Portugal. Maria II. 5 Reis. Uncirculated. Bright red. .25.
Patagonia. Orille-Antoine I. 1874. 2 Centavos. Proof. .50.
Paraguay. 1-12. Lion. Very fine. .40.
Portuguese Africa. ½, 1 Macuta. Very fine. 1 25.
Papal States. Pius IX. 4 Soldi. Bright. .50. Extra fine olive. .35.
Papal States. Gregory XVI. and Pius IX. Baiocco. Uncirculated. Bright. .75.
Poland. 1831. 3 Grosze. Uncirculated. Brilliant red. .25.
Roman Republic. 40. 4 Baiocchi. Base silver. Very fine and uncirculated. 1.50.
Roman Republic. 3 Baiocchi. Uncirculated. Bright red. 1.00.
Roumania. 5, 10 Bani. Extremely fine. .50.
Russia. 1775-1805. 5 Kopecs. Weight, 2 oz. Very fine. .50. Good. .35.
Sierra Leone. Prowling lion. 1791. Cent. Bronze proof. .75.
Sarawak. Cent. Bright. 1.00. Fine. .50.
Sandwich Islands. Kamehameha III. Hapi Haneri. Uncirculated. Bright red. .75. Fine. .50.
St. Martin. ¼ R. Fine. .35.
Siberia. 1764. Sable Foxes. Set of 10, 5, 2, 1, ¼ Kopec, the latter very scarce. Very fine. 7.50.
Siberia. 1796. Magnificent set of rare patterns. Obverse, crowned monogram of the emperor surrounded by raised dots denoting the value—a Russian device to help the illiterate. 10, 5, 4, 2, 1, ½, ¼ Kopec, with edge varieties of 5, 4 and 2 Kopecs. The 10 kopec of this set is larger than that with the sable foxes. Beautiful brilliant red, or handsomer light bronze proofs. 10 pcs. 25.00.
Suriname. 1764. Coffee plant. About uncirculated. 1.00.
Sweden. Large Or's. Size 30. 1677-1685. Fine. Each. .75.
States of Jersey. 1888. 1-12, 1-24 Sh. Uncirculated. Bright red. .35.
Sicily. 1849. Ferd. II. ½, 1, 1½, 2 Tornese. Uncirculated. Bright red. 1.25.
Sicily under Napoleon. Head of Jerome Napoleon. 3 Grana. Good. .75.
Strasburg. Siege Decime. 1814-1815. L and N crowned. Fine. Pair. .75.
St. Helena. Halfpenny. Very good. .20.

Augsburg, Brunswick, Rostock, Anhalt, Achen, Mecklenburg, Heuneburg, Hamm, Nassau, Hohenzollern, Lippe, Hesse-Darmstadt, Saxe-Meiningen, Oldenburg, etc. Some in 1600. Bear, Griffin, Horse, Ox-head, Lion, Hen, Snipe, Pine-cone, Rose, Wheel, etc. All different. A very fine lot, 25 uncirculated. 180 pieces. 15.00.

War Medals.

United States. Silver medal presented to John Bowen, by City of New York for the war with Mexico. Arms of New York, rev., typical female pointing to city and harbor—Cerro Gordo—Chapultepec—Cherubusco—Vera Cruz. Very fine. Size 32. Weight 2 oz. Av. 6.00.

Silver medal presented by South Carolina to Palmetto Regiment, Mexican War. Palmetto tree; rev., troops landing from boats. Silver, ribbon attached. Very fine. Size 31. 7.50.

Same. Tin, ribbon attached. Very fine. 2.00.

Shield-shaped badge. Wreath enclosing cactus, fort, "Mexico 1846;" above, ship, arms and cannon, names of battles around edge. Unused. Bronze. Size 33 x36. 5.00.

"Death to traitors;" medal of the Iron Brigade, N. Y. Vol's; white metal, ribbon attached. Good. Size 24. 1.00.

West Virginia. Liberty crowning a soldier, 1861-1865. Copper. Uncirculated. 3.00. Very good. 1.50.

Austria. Maltese cross for 25 years service, F. W. III. under crown in centre; rev., XXV in centre; gilt, ribbon attached. Size 24. Perfect. 2.00.

Anhalt. Shield of arms crowned; rev., bear walking on wall. Order of "Albert the Bear," bronze proof. Size 20. 1.25.

England. Waterloo medal. Bust of Prince Regent; rev., Victory seated, "Wellington" above, "Waterloo, June 18, 1815" below. Silver, light scratches on obverse, ribbon attached. 5.00.

The following English medals all have head of Victoria on obverse and are silver of size 24 unless otherwise described.

"Ava." Rev., Victory seated; "To the Army of India, 1799-1826." Bar, "Ava," ribbon attached. Very fine. 5.00.

Army of Punjab. Rev., soldiers surrendering to mounted British officers. 1849. Two bars, "Mooltan and Goojerat," ribbon attached. Very fine. 6.00.

"Northwest Frontier." Rev., Victory crowning a naked warrior. Bar, "Northwest Frontier," ribbon attached. Very fine. 5.00.

"Pegu." Same reverse. Bar, "Pegu." Very fine. 3.50.

"Umbeyla." Same reverse. Bar, "Umbeyla." Very fine. 5.00.

Crimea. Four bars. "Alma, Balaklava, Inkermann, Sebastapol," ribbon attached. Very fine. 15.00.

Crimea. Rev., flying Victory placing wreath on warrior in Roman costume, "Crimea" in field. Three bars, "Sebastopol, Inkermann, Alma," ribbon attached. Very fine. 10.00.

Same. One bar, "Sebastopol," ribbon attached, very fine. 4.00. Another without bar but with swivel and ribbon, very fine. 3.00. Another, no bar or ribbon, very fine. 2.50.

India, 1857-58. Rev., Una and the lion. Bar, "Delhi," ribbon attached. Semiproof. Rare. 6.00.

India, 1857-58. Same reverse. Bar, Lucknow. Very fine. 4.00.

India, 1857-58. Same reverse. Swivel and ribbon. Very fine. 3.00.

India, 1857-58. Same reverse. Bar, "Central India." Very fine. 4.00.

India, 1857-58. Same reverse. Two bars, "Lucknow," "Defense of Lucknow," ribbon attached. Fine. 6.00.

Baltic, 1854-55. Rev., Britannia seated, two fortresses in background. Bar and ribbon. Proof. 3.50.

China. Rev., trophy of arms, flags, etc., "China" below. Two bars, "Pekin 1860 and Taku Forts 1860," ribbon attached. Fine. 5.00.

South Africa. Rev., Lion and bush, "South Africa" above. Bar, "1879," ribbon attached. Very fine. 3.50.

Arctic Discoveries. Rev., Arctic scene, 1818–1855. Octagon; ribbon attached. Very fine. Size 22. Rare. 4.00.

1848. Rev., Victory crowning Wellington, "To the British Army, 1793–1814." Bar, "Badajoz," ribbon attached. Very fine. Rare. 6.00.

New Zealand. Head crowned, veil falling down behind; rev., wreath, "New Zealand Virtutis Honor." Ornamented bar and ribbon. Very fine. 4.00.

Abyssinia. Crowned and veiled head in centre of large star, between the points, "Abyssinia;" rev., name of wearer in wreath. Crown and ring with ribbon above. Semi-proof. Size 22. 5.00.

Veiled head of Victoria; rev., a number of semi-nude Ashantees fighting in bush with infantry. Bar and ribbon. Very fine. 3.50.

Egypt. Soudan. Bust of Queen; rev., sphinx. Bar, "El-teb-tamaai," ribbon attached. Fine proof. 6.00.

Egypt. Same design. Bar, "The Nile, 1884–85," ribbon attached. Fine proof. 6.00.

Egypt. Same design. Bar, "Suakim, 1885." Proof. 6.00.

Egypt. Same design. Bar, "Tel-el-kebir," ribbon attached. Fine proof. 6.00.

Bust of Queen; rev., sphinx, 1882, Egypt. Bar, "Tel-el-kebir," ribbon attached. Officers' medal. Semi-proof. Size 12. 3.00.

Afghanistan. Rev., elephant artillery. Bar "Ali Musjid," ribbon attached. Semi-proof. 6.00. Another, plain bar, with ribbon. Proof. 4.00.

Afghanistan. Same design. Bar, "Ahmed Khel," ribbon attached. Fine proof. 6.00.

Persia. Rev., Victory crowning Roman warrior. Bar, "Persia." Fine proof. 6.00.

Sutlej Campaign. Rev., Victory standing holding wreath, war trophies at her feet, Moodkee, 1845, below. Three bars, "Sobraon, Aliwal, Ferozeshuhur." Proof. 10.00.

Syria. 1848. Rev., Britannia seated on hippocampus. Bar, "Syria," ribbon attached. Brilliant proof. 6.00.

Coat of Arms; rev., "For long service and good conduct." Bar with ribbon. Proof. 4.00.

Star of five points, in centre sphinx and pyramids, "Egypt 1882." Rev., crowned monogram. Bar with star and crescent, ribbon attached. Given to English soldiers who served during the war against Arabi Pasha. Perfect. Bronze. Size 30. 3.50.

France. Napoleon III. Expedition to China, 1860. Head. Rev., names of battles. Ribbon with Chinese characters attached. Silver. Size 20. Unused. 3.50.

Same. Officers' size. With ribbon. Unused. Size 11. 2.50.

Same. Unused. Size 7. 1.50.

Napoleon III. For Mexican campaign. 1862–1863. Silver. Very fine. Ribbon attached. Size 20. 2.50.

Republic. Expedition to China, 1883–1885. Rev., names of battles. Silver. Size 20. Unused. 3.00.

Prussia. 1870–1871. W. crowned. Gilt. Very fine. Size 19. .35.

Saxe-Gotha-Altenburg. The Altenburg rose; rev., ducal crown. Bronze. Very fine. Size 27. 1.00.

Turkey. For Crimea, 1855. Trophy of cannon, etc.; rev., cipher of Abdul Medjid. Silver. Size 24. Very fine. 2.00.

Numismatic Books and Pamphlets.

Steigerwalt's Illustrated History of United States and Colonial Coins. Many illustrations and the cheapest work of its class. Cloth. .75. Stiff paper covers, .50.

"Early Half Dimes," Harold P. Newlin, 1883. Full descriptions of the varieties of the early dates and also an interesting article on the whereabouts of all the known 1802 Half Dimes. Fine paper with broad margins. New. Edition very limited. Cloth. 1.00. Paper, .50.

Madden's History of Jewish coinages. Many illustrations. 350 pages. Half mo-
rocco. New and uncut. 5.00.
Atlas Numismatique du Canada. Jos. Le Roux. 1883. 40 pages, with illustrations
of all the 220 Canadian coins. Letter press in English and French. A
valuable work. Paper covers. 1.00.
Coin Collectors' Manual. Jones. 1860. .50.
Silver coins of England. Henry. 1878. ,48 pages. Illustrated pamphlet. .35.
Numisgraphics or a list of sale catalogues. Atinnelli, 1876. 134 pages. Paper
covers. Rare. 2.00.
Haseltine's " Paper Money of the Colonies." Illustrated. Pamphlet. .25.
Haseltine's " Confederate Notes and Bonds." .25.
" Das Romische Ass." German. 24 pages. 6 plates. .35.
The Naturalist's Directory. Cassino. 1886. 4801 names. 1.00.
Historia Numorum. A Manual of Greek Numismatics by Barclay V. Head, Assistant
Keeper of the Department of Coins and Medals in the British Museum.
1887. Hundreds of illustrations. 818 pages. Half morocco. By far the
best work of its class ever issued. 12.50.
Coins, medals and seals. W. C. Prime. 114 plates. 292 pages. Cloth. New
York, 1861. 3.50.
Silver coins of England. Hawkins. 308 pages. 47 plates. Half Morocco. Lon-
don. 1841. 3.50.
Coins of the Grand Master of Malta. R. Morris, Boston, 1884. 6 plates. 70 pages.
Cloth. 1.50.
The coinage of Morelos. Illustrated 4to. pamphlet. Privately printed. 18 pages.
N. Y., 1886. .50.
American Journal of Numismatics. Vol. 1 to Vol. 9, No. 1 bound in two vol's,
one half, and the other full morocco. Vol. 9, No. 2 to Vol. 14, (excepting
13 No. 4, and 14 No. 4), Vol. 17, 18, 19, No. 1 and 2, unbound. The two
missing numbers, Vol. 15 and 16, and late issues (now in 25th Vol.), can be
supplied, if desired, at $2 per Vol. to complete set. 25.00.

Curiosities.

Knight of Pythias sword. Handsome steel scabbard and mountings. Knights, Pil-
grims, Eagles, etc. Very fine and desirable. Probably made for an officer
and cost about $30. Uninjured by use. In buckskin cover. 10.00.
A single hair from the head of Henry Clay. Taken when the body was lying in
state at Baltimore. .50.
Agate egg. Full size of a hen's egg. Very handsome. 1.50.
Massive brown agate paper weight, in shape of a seal and handle, cut from one
piece. Very handsome and valuable. 5¾ inches long, 2¾ inches wide
at top. 5.00.
Seal. Similar. Red agate. 2⅛ inches long. Handsome. 2.50.
Marble paper weight. " Appian Way," near Ravenna, Italy. .75.
Bohemian glass, beads and specimens of. 20 pieces. Lot for 1.00.
Egyptian scarabeus. Very fine. 1.50.
Olive wood pipe. Liberty bell design. New. .50.
Paper weight. Glass. View of foreign building. 3 inches. .50.
Japan. Native painted photo. on glass in case. Very odd. 1.00.
Japan. Opium pipe. New. .75.
Piece of gold ore, oval, polished ready for mounting as a breast pin. Size 26. 5.00.
Agatized wood, partially coated with amethyst crystals. Cross section of tree. One
face polished, the other rough. 6x7 in. 3 in. thick. Beautiful specimen,
the polishing alone cost nearly $10. 7.50.
Jasperized wood, shows the bark distinctly. Cross section of tree. One side pol-
ished, the other rough. 7x8 in. 2 in. thick. As handsome as last. 7.50.
Ostrich egg. South Africa. Fine large specimen. 2.50.
Fine specimen of amber with insect enclosed. Rare. 1.50. Smaller. 1.00.
Silver female, Peruvian figure with long hair. Hung, with prayer, on the figure of
the Virgin for the cure of disease. 1¾ inches. Rare. 2.00.

Indian doe-skin slipper. Fancy bead work. Very fine. 1.00.

Pottery vase and ball stopper from Cyprus. Old and valuable. 2.00.

Aztec Idol, carved from pumice stone, prehistoric, very fine specimen, dug from mound near Durango, Mexico. 15x9x7 inches. Very desirable. 100.00.

Hindoo Idol. Fine white marble. Old. 16 x 9½ in. 25.00.

Old Japanese. God of Plenty. Very odd. Bronze. 6 x 4 in. 10.00.

Old Japanese. Dog Foy on stump. Bronze. 4 x 4 in. 10.00.

Small wooden figure of elephant, ivory tusks, 2½ in. 1.50.

Ivory queen, black, elaborately carved dress. 3.00.

Ancient bronze statuette. Venus. 2½ in. From Syria. 3.00.

Ancient bronze statuette. Curious animal. 1½ in. From Syria. 2.00.

Ancient Roman spearhead, iron, 3½ in. From German Mound. 2.00.

Terra Vert Ancient Egyptian ornaments, Lion, Anubias, etc. 5 pcs. Lot for 7.50.

Plumes of the Egret or White Crane, snow white, 22 in., Florida. 2.00.

Skin of Mottled Crane, very fine, 27 in., Florida. 1.50.

Petrified jawbone with teeth. .50.

Curious polished stone, natural scene resembling a river and bank with trees and foliage. 10½ in. 5.00.

Remarkable clay idol from Guatemala. Human figure with tail. Head broken from body (has been mended), and part of legs missing. Curious and rare. 2.50.

Florida sea-beans. 14 pcs. .75.

Beautiful polished section of elephant tusk. 5¼x6 in. 3.50.

Gourd Dish. From Peruvian mound. Fine. 1.00.

Brazil. Nut-case filled with nuts. 4x4. 2.00.

Swedish Plate Money.

1720–1738. ½, 1, 2, 4 Daler. A fine set of this curious money. The 4 Daler is 9 inches square, and weighs 9 pounds. Set cheap at 30.00.